Life Reimagined

Leave Chaos Behind
Find Balance
Thrive

Jason L. Ranck

with Shawn Smucker

Co-written with Shawn Smucker
Edited by Barbara Gerhart and Andi Cumbo
Cover Design by Brenna Ryan
Back cover photos by Aleesha Nicole Howe

To my dear wife Angie,
the bravest person I know,
for never giving up on me
and for persevering
in your fight for health.

Table of Contents

PART ONE: OUR STORY

PART TWO: BUILDING A BALANCED LIFE

PART THREE: YOU GOT THIS

Part One
Our Story

Chapter One
Building Passion for a
Balanced Life

Most of us have two different lives.

There is the life we live now, unbalanced and hectic, in which we run from one thing to another. In this life, we are stressed out, anxious, and dissatisfied. Our relationships are never quite what they could be. But instead of sitting down and acknowledging our unhappiness, we get busier. We commit to more things. We keep moving.

This way, we don't have to think about what we're missing.

But there is another life.

In this life, we are balanced. We know who we are and why we're here. We make better decisions about our spiritual, emotional, relational, and mental health. We set clear boundaries. When our relationships suffer, we take time to address the deep issues instead of patching them quickly and moving on.

But often, that second life seems so unattainable. So distant.

It seemed that way for me.

At one point, my wife's health was at rock-bottom as was our relationship. I was nearing burnout at work. Life felt completely overwhelming.

What would it take for you to move into a more balanced life, a happier life, a more meaningful life?

For me, it took much less than I expected.

We actually pulled this off.

I was sitting outside a small café on the boardwalk at Bethany Beach in April with my two boys. The morning sun glimmered off the Atlantic, and a cool breeze tugged at the napkins on the table. It was around 9 a.m., and I was drinking tea while the kids ate a late breakfast. My wife Angie was back at the beach house getting some much-needed rest.

My work email was turned off, the office at home was running well without me, and I was fully engaged in this time with my boys. I had finally learned to dial back the chaos that had nearly destroyed my marriage and my life. Best of all, we had worked out how to fit a five-week stay at the beach into our schedule. Granted, I couldn't be there for all five weeks, but we planned it out so I could spend long weekends there as well as one complete week.

It was the spring we all needed.

The kids finished up their waffles and yogurt parfaits, and we got back on our bikes and rode away. It was 75 degrees and sunny, and it felt like we were living the life I had always dreamed about, the life I wanted but didn't think I would see for another 20 years.

We all have an image in our minds of what our dream lives look like. What is yours? Where are you in this dream life? What are you tasting, smelling, seeing? Take a moment to write it out. What is the life you always wanted?

You can get there. It's completely possible. In fact, it exists right now, but it's hidden under layers of misconceptions, habits, or patterns that need to change—like your inability to separate work from family time or a skewed perspective on your identity. It may need to change at the spiritual level. It may require going deeper and listening more intently for the voice of God.

Are you willing to try something new, something that will challenge you, stretch you, push you in a good direction, even if it makes you uncomfortable? Are you willing to set boundaries and make time for the things you don't think you have time for?

I know what it means to be overwhelmed by life and the direction it is going. I was going into work on minimal sleep, existing in a dying marriage that was unfulfilling for both my wife and me, battling an addiction that ate at me from the inside, and struggled through days that slipped through my fingers. My wife was very ill, and we saw no light at the end of the tunnel.

After long days at work, I came home to a place that I knew would be a wreck, physically and emotionally. Because of her ongoing medical condition, Angie did not have the energy to function well. She was doing all she could to literally stay alive, and I supported her in that. So as I walked through our front door every evening, I expected to find her on the couch, sick, exhausted, and in pain. The laundry and dishes would be piled up and waiting for me. My boys needed me. And even after I finished all the housework, I knew I'd be up most of the night with my son Colton, helping him fight his asthma attacks by administering breathing treatments.

I regularly wondered, *How can I keep this up?*

How can I survive this pace?

How did I end up in this life?

But when those questions surfaced, I pushed them down. After all, what was the point in even pondering the questions when I didn't have any answers? I put my head down, tried to be a presence for my boys, and kept moving forward as best as I could. I helped my wife cope with life and her illness, but if I'm honest, I blamed her condition for the state of our life. I thought that if we could get her healthy, our problems would be solved. The reality was that while her sickness certainly influenced our life together, our problems actually had much deeper roots.

Maybe this is where you're at. You feel like your marriage is at a dead end or your work is taking over your life. You're doing your best to cope, but you've lost any sense that things could be better.

You've lost hope.

But there is hope. During those years, going through what felt like hell on earth, not only did I keep my job, but I was promoted to general manager at a fast-paced, growing, service-based company. My wife is now on her way back to complete health, making progress every year. Our marriage is strong. And we found a way to slow down the pace of life, to enjoy it, to enjoy each other. We're living the life we always wanted to live, and getting there only required a few small but crucial adjustments.

Before I tell you the rest of my story, I want to encourage you with two things:

Don't give up on your dreams.

Be prepared to make some adjustments.

Chapter Two
The Bottom

In March 2014, I took my wife Angie into the hospital. She had been declining in health for about a year, battling ulcerative colitis and clostridium difficile infections (or C. diff). She would take the medication for C. diff and it would go away, but that caused the ulcerative colitis to flare up. Four or five weeks later, after the ulcerative colitis eased, the C. diff returned. This happened for six cycles, and the toll it took on her body was brutal. She had nothing left: no energy, no strength, no will to fight.

Angie had been diagnosed in her teens with ulcerative colitis, an inflammatory bowel disease that causes long-lasting inflammation and ulcers (sores) in your digestive tract and drains you of energy.

This time, she was also diagnosed with C. diff, a bacterium that can cause symptoms ranging from diarrhea to life-threatening inflammation in the colon that is very hard to fight by itself let alone with another illness in the colon like ulcerative colitis. Her body fought hard but struggled to stay ahead of the battle raging in her gut, and over time, these things took their toll on her to the point she couldn't function.

She barely had the strength to wake up some days, and that's when it all fell on me. Those were the days when I couldn't see a way out.

One evening, I came home from work, exhausted as usual. I walked in to find Angie's sister there beside the couch. Angie was in and out of consciousness. Mentally, she wasn't with it. Her vital signs were still there, but her body had begun shutting down because of infections and pain. We later found out she was in the early stages of sepsis, a life-threatening condition that arises when the body's response to infection causes injury to its own tissues and organs as well as mental confusion. The struggle had become too much, and she could no longer function.

At 8 p.m. on a Friday night, I rushed her to the

hospital. The kids were at her sister's house where they had spent most of their time during the past three months due to Angie's health. We checked into the ER, but there wasn't much the hospital staff could do besides hydrate her. She needed the fluids, but they had no magic wand to get rid of the infection. We were there for only a short time when they told me they wanted to discharge her.

"She's just dehydrated," they said, trying to explain away her symptoms. They gave us a few more hours, but by 2 or 3 a.m., they said we needed to go home.

"We don't know what else to do for you," one of the doctors said.

Later, Angie would remember that night through a thick fog. She was in and out. She wondered if she was having seizures, what was happening. But she had a sense that her body was shutting down, and she didn't even have the strength to speak. She was in constant, terrible pain.

She thought she was going to die.

I did, too. I thought I was losing her. I thought we were close to the end.

Despite her condition, Angie and I had to leave the hospital. Her primary doctors were out of town, so we had no one to speak on our behalf, no one to explain what was wrong, to advocate for her or explain what she needed. It was 3 a.m., and we stopped at a pharmacy on the way home to grab what we could in order to hydrate her and get her through the weekend. These were mostly over-the-counter treatments recommended by the hospital staff as they had ushered us out the door.

At home, neither of us could sleep. She had chronic stomach cramping but nothing left to pass. She wasn't eating. She wasn't sleeping. Saturday and Sunday crept by, and nothing changed, except perhaps that she was getting worse

I didn't know what to do.

On Monday morning, my mom came over to be with Angie, and I went to work because that's all I knew. We had been in this struggle for years, and I was used to continuing on no matter what. I secretly expected that at some point I'd have to head home and take her back to the emergency room. She looked awful as I walked out the front door. I tried to stay coherent at work, lining things up so that I could leave when I needed to.

My mom called at 2 p.m.

"You need to take her back to the hospital," she said. "She's getting worse again." I left work and went home, only to find Angie battling seizure-like symptoms. Angie's sister came and picked up the kids. My mom and I helped Angie into the car and headed to the Reading Hospital. I thought we might get better support at a different hospital. I was at the end of my rope, willing to try anything.

On our way there, she had a massive seizure. *This is it*, I thought. *This is the moment Angie dies.* But she held on.

Physically getting her inside the hospital was a challenge since she didn't have the strength to walk and could barely hold her head up. By then, Angie was incoherent. She could barely respond to the nurses' questions. It was the tail-end of Saint Patrick's Day weekend, and I think a few nurses suspected she was drunk or high.

They kept delaying, telling me, "Okay, hang in there. We'll get to you."

I was filling out paperwork at the front desk, with

Angie in a wheelchair beside me, when she suddenly slumped over. She was unconscious. They immediately moved her to the front of the waiting line, gave her a bed, and started checking her out. They worked hard to hydrate her while they figured out a long-term treatment plan. All the ER rooms were taken, so they tried to stabilize her in the ER hallway. The entire time I'm wondering, *Is this it?*

Is this the day I lose my wife?

We waited in the hospital that afternoon for five or six hours, hoping the fluids would help her improve, and just as an ER doctor came to look at her, she had another terrible seizure. He immediately moved her into the acute section of the ER. She was now in and out of unconsciousness, very slow to respond to the nurses' questions, and hooked up to fluids through an IV. They started running CAT scans checking for brain damage. They worked hard to diagnose her so that they could admit her.

Eventually, at around 4 a.m., they admitted her, gave her a room, began administering pain medication, and things quieted down. We still didn't have many answers, but Angie seemed to have stabilized in her critical state, and now we could begin trying to figure out how to help her recover and heal. It felt like we had a long journey ahead of us.

Angie told me that on that night she reached the point where she was ready to give up. Her father had passed away four years before, and she thought it would be better to die and be with her dad than to continue living in that kind of pain. She didn't care anymore. She was ready to go.

Then, in the middle of this unconscious state, she saw her dad.

He leaned in close and said, "Angie, don't give up. Fight. Your husband needs you, and your boys need you."

Fight.

She returned from the darkness enough to realize where she was and to see me there beside her bed, crying, facing the reality that my future might not include her.

"Don't," she said in a weak voice. "Don't cry. I need you to be strong for me." This was the bottom.

From there, we could only go up.

Chapter Three
The Heart of the Matter

I did my best to separate my work and home life in those days and thought I'd done a fairly good job. I couldn't be in two places at once: when I was at work, I busted my butt, and when I was home, I tried to be present and take care of a mountain of responsibilities. But I was burning out.

The mental stress of Angie's health situation combined with carrying most of the work at home, all on minimal hours of sleep each night, caused emotional fractures to form. I was getting close to a collapse.

Around the time we were married, I had made a commitment to Angie that I would go to every doctor's appointment she ever had. During this episode, when I thought I was losing her, she spent eight days in the hospital, and I didn't go to work the entire time. It became an eight-day period when I started putting my own life together again. I asked myself some tough questions, and I wasn't just thinking about Angie's health, though that was at the top of my list.

How do we get Angie better?

How do we get better as a couple?

How do we get better as a family?

How do I get better as a father, a husband, and an employee?

Where do we go from here?

During those eight days, I realized we weren't a family anymore, and while this was mostly due to the health issues we were facing, I still felt like at the heart level there were things we could change to improve our lives as a family.

The kids were always at someone else's house. I went out to see them at one point, stopping by Angie's sister's house, and I saw them running around and playing and interacting with other adults. I sat down at her sister's kitchen table and wept. My boys' mom was in the hospital, I was losing it emotionally, and they were getting on with life without us. It felt like if I didn't do something, we would all go our separate ways.

What had happened to my family? How could I get them back again?

After Angie was released from the hospital, I returned to work, but during those eight days, I had asked a lot of questions and reevaluated my life. And this reevaluation led me to question my habits and my approach to life. Up until that point, my mindset was that I would work as hard as I could until I was 45 or 50 years old, and hopefully by then I'd be in a good position financially, able to live a comfortable life without working so hard. I'd have more time with my family, take more vacations, and spend weekends at home instead of the office. I'd find a more centered way. But to get to this point, I would work my tail off for the next 15 years or so and then be prepared to enjoy the good life Angie and I dreamed about.

But during that hospital stay, I began thinking there had to be a better way. We were guaranteed nothing! What if I worked like a madman until I was 40 and then dropped dead with a coronary? What if

Angie didn't live that long? The future was not promised to either of us.

There had to be a more balanced way of living, starting now. I wondered if there was a way to have an amazing family life and still work hard and be successful. It had to be possible to build both wealth and a healthy family without compromising!

I started looking around, and some of the successful people I saw in their 50s confirmed my fears. They made it through the crazy time of life, building their careers, raising their children. They hit the empty nest. But once they reached the "golden years," they didn't seem to connect with their spouses anymore. It was like the habits they created while putting most of their energy into building their careers had become a way of life they could not break out of. They had the career success I was chasing, but slowing down and enjoying what they had built was proving too big of a challenge.

What's the point of building companies and fulfilling life-long career dreams if that's all that's waiting for me at the end? Is it possible to build this career success and enjoy my family at the same time?

I decided I would try to find out.

Life Reimagined

Part Two
Building a
Balanced Life

Life Reimagined

Chapter Four
Who are You?

As I tried to discover better paths to success, I quickly realized something crucial: my work had become my identity. As I stripped work away from other parts of my life, I sensed an even bigger, deeper question.

Who was I?

It's a scary question to ask at 31 years of age when you suddenly realize the things you used to find your identity in no longer apply. Before placing boundaries between my work and the rest of my life, when the job infiltrated everything, it was easy to believe that was who I was. Jason, the hard worker. Jason, the guy making lots of money. If I continued to succeed at work, I was a successful person. Help my employers grow their company, and people would say good things about me. Everyone would respect me, and they would listen when I spoke.

But as I strained work out from the rest of my life, I realized my career wasn't all of who I was. Sure, work will always define part of who I am, but it's not the entirety of my existence, and it could change in the blink of an eye. If I could no longer perform or if I was asked to leave, that part of my identity would be gone in an instant.

It didn't seem wise to build my identity on something that wouldn't last. I knew I wanted to "seek first the kingdom of God," but the reality was I was seeking first money and power. I wasn't seeking God's approval—I was following my own ambition, my own goals.

The reality is that, no matter where I'm employed, my true identity is found in Christ's love for me. God will continue to give me gifts and opportunities to help further his kingdom, but if my identity is only wrapped up in those things, I have grounded myself in something that will not last forever.

I remember one of the goals I had before searching for my true identity was to be making a six-digit annual income by the time I was thirty years old. Then, I did it, and you know what? I have never had an accomplished goal feel so pointless.

With that goal, my identity quickly centered around how much money I could make. My goals and, as a result, my identity had nothing to do with how my life was bringing glory to God. The financial goal was not wrong in and of itself, but the reasons behind it— making more money and making me look better— were too shallow.

Pornography had also begun owning my life, and I battled hard to beat the addiction. The combined stress and loneliness that came from fighting Angie's illness, running the house on my own, and working myself into exhaustion paved the way for me to turn to porn as a way out of my life.

I knew I needed to find a way to beat porn and build a healthy relationship with power and money if I was going to be able to find my true identity and build a strong spiritual relationship with Christ.

I started probing my spiritual life.

Where could I give more time to pursuing God

and his thoughts? What could I practically apply to my Christian walk that would improve my spiritual life?

I started taking prayer walks every other Tuesday afternoon. I put it on my calendar, and I decided I was going to be there. No one would interfere with that time. I kept a journal listing things I was thankful for, how I saw God work, and what God was saying to me.

These simple times of quiet brought incredible clarity to my life. It's not that I prayed during the entire walk, though that was part of it. I simply talked with God about the big stuff going on in my life, and sometimes that meant praying out loud. At other times, it meant listening. Sometimes it was just walking, breathing in fresh air and giving myself space to think and process.

Through all this, I started learning so much about what it meant to be in a relationship with God, to listen, to take the next step and follow even when I didn't know what the future held.

It rocked my identity at its core, but I was beginning to understand that if I was going to make any meaningful changes within our marriage or in my career, those changes needed to start with who I was at a heart level.

My identity.

Soon after I started taking prayer walks, our marriage was hit hard by things that could have divided us. In the past, these *would* have divided us. But because our family life was stronger, because these prayer walks gave me more clarity, Angie and I weren't divided.

Another benefit was that as Angie saw the effort I was making, she grew more confident in me as a husband, a father, and a leader. She was impressed that I was willing to step up spiritually, to dedicate myself to seeking God, and this strengthened us as a couple. We began praying together more often.

One night, as we talked through these tough things, she said, "The devil has to go through you now in order to get to me."

I was blown away. I wasn't living a perfect life. I struggled with things that I just couldn't seem to get past, things that could potentially wreck our lives. Yet, Angie and the devil both knew where I stood, and the path I was on was victory in Christ.

You have no excuses not to be a spiritual warrior for your family.

Angie's confidence in me continued to grow

simply because she saw me investing in things that strengthened our family, our relationship, and my walk with God.

So, what does a prayer walk look like?

It's pretty simple. I go to a local park up in the woods. On average, I'm there 30 to 45 minutes. Sometimes, I hike through the woods, enjoying the physical activity. Sometimes, I stand there talking out loud to myself or to God.

At other times, I sit and wait for God to speak, and my mind's not even on prayer, but he's giving me clarity in a specific area. When I go determined to hear from God, he puts things on my mind that I need to think about. It's a time to reset, to be thankful, and to reach out to God about what's pressing in around me.

Sometimes, I'll be there 10 or 15 minutes and realize, on that day, I'm just there to listen. Nothing more. And maybe God isn't even going to say anything. Maybe it's just time to take a breather, to hang out, to relax. God is always there, but sometimes he's not giving me any significant revelation or specific direction. The time becomes a quiet hang-out session, and those are the most amazing walks. Those times remind me of what real relationships are like. God is saying, "I don't have to talk every time. There doesn't have to be something pressing or important going on in your life for us to hang out together. Be who you were created to be. Enjoy that."

After the walk, I always journal, and this is crucial because it allows me to put down in concrete fashion what I'm hearing. Then, as the days and weeks pass, I can look back and see how God was speaking to me, what he has said in the past, and the direction he's been leading me.

I connect with God spiritually in many ways, but I have found over time these prayer walks are the glue that holds everything together. They're when God and I hash things out, build a better relationship, and I can receive his strength, helping me to power into the future.

I read this recently in the book *Jesus Calling*, and it summed up so much of what I experienced as I sought to connect with God on a deeper level and find my true identity:

True dependence is not simply asking Me[God] to bless what you have decided to do. It is coming to Me with an open mind and heart, inviting Me to plant my desires within you. I may infuse within you a dream that seems far beyond your reach. You know that in yourself you cannot achieve such a goal. Thus, begins your journey of profound reliance on Me. It is a faith-walk, taken one step at a time, leaning on Me as much as you need.

Going deeper spiritually made all the difference when it came to finding my identity and moving closer to the "other life" I knew was out there. Creating a quiet space, my prayer walks, helped me to wrestle with who I truly was. Building a stronger relationship with God brought massive power and benefits into my life that I didn't even know existed.

What is your identity? Can you set it aside and make room for silence in your life? Are you brave enough to surround yourself with people who will help you find your way? What are your goals, and why are they important to you?

The journey to finding your identity will put you squarely on the journey to finding a better life.

Chapter Five
Marriage

I met Angie through her sister and brother-in-law when a group of us guys were hanging out at their house. She made an impression on me, so I called her one night out of the blue to ask her out. We went out, had coffee, and proceeded to have three of the most awkward dates in history.

After those three outings, we mutually decided this was not working for us, but I remember hanging up the phone and thinking, *This girl is perfect. I'm going to marry her.*

A few years later, our paths crossed again when I started going to her church's young adult group. We eventually began dating again and were married 10 months later.

The time we were dating was a lot of fun. We were madly in love, and we were completely content simply hanging out with each other. Her dad had been diagnosed with stage four cancer a year or so before we began dating, and no one knew how much longer he'd be around, so it was pretty common for us to go out for coffee then spend the rest of the evening with her family at their place.

Angie was well when we first got married and not experiencing any health issues. We had a good marriage during those early years. We were learning to love each other and build a strong relationship. After our first son, Carter, was born, her health issues began. He arrived in November of 2010, and she had a minor intestinal flare-up early the next year. Our second son was born in January 2013, and by April of that year, she started getting heavy symptoms. She went downhill fast.

Our marriage hit rock bottom at about the same time Angie's health did. After the hospital stay where I thought she was going to die and even after she started making measurable progress, the two of us were still drifting apart.

In the early days of her recovery, I was still coming home to laundry, making supper, cleaning the house, washing the dishes, getting up with the kids in the night, and then heading off to work on minimal hours of sleep. Angie's physical health had stabilized, but emotionally she still struggled. She drifted into depression. We felt alone on the journey even though both of our families were continuing to help out as they could and we had hired a lady from church to help with chores and play with the boys one day a week. But we were tired of being sick. Tired of being tired. We didn't want it to be like that anymore.

Another reality was that Angie's journey back to health was becoming extremely expensive. We decided to try a few natural options, and they added to the financial load, bringing on additional bills. In my heart, I knew every dollar spent was worth it, but we still disagreed from time to time on what to try. When we took the time to talk about the various options, we usually ended up misunderstanding each other, further complicating our relationship.

I fought to stay even-keeled with my emotions. I tried to keep one eye on our budget, practically speaking. But my way of caring for Angie was going along to her appointments, paying the bills, and keeping our finances balanced. She was sick, and I was loving her the best way I knew how, but it wasn't the kind of compassion she needed.

I was taking care of the logistics, but I wasn't taking care of her heart. Our marriage wasn't where it was supposed to be. We teetered on the brink of disaster.

Everything came to a head one night at 1 a.m. while we were packing for a weekend with extended family. I was tentatively asking some questions about our relationship, but she kept asking what kind of cookies we should take on the trip. It felt like I was banging my head up against a brick wall!

She didn't want to talk about it. She didn't want to verbalize just how bad things had become between us. But for some reason on that night, I knew we needed to talk, so I kept pressing her.

"Stop talking about cookies! We need to talk about our marriage!" I insisted. "We have to stop avoiding this."

She stared at me and gave in. All these walls she had built up over the years suddenly collapsed, and she decided to be completely honest. "I've been hurt so bad by you that I don't know if I can ever love you again."

What do you do with that kind of statement?

"I'm never going to leave you," she continued quietly, "but I don't know if I can love you again."

I was stunned into silence, devastated, wondering what to do with this. How did we get here? She had survived the worst health crisis of her life; I sat beside her the entire time, yet all along our marriage had been dying with no one paying attention to its long, slow decline. What did this mean for us? And what's the point of living in the same house with someone who doesn't know if they can ever love you again?

"Has this all been for nothing?" I asked her. "All these years, all this effort? We've got two young kids. We've made it through the worst of your health issues. I'm working so hard to keep us afloat. Has it all been for nothing?"

Angie stared at me. "I know we've done all of these things. I know you've worked hard, and I appreciate everything. I just feel like you don't know how to get to my heart," she said, tears welling up in her eyes.

Inside, I felt myself getting defensive. I was hurt by what she said, and I wondered if I could forgive her for not caring about the ways I thought I was loving her. I could only think of all I had done: paying the bills, working hard, staying by her side for eight days in the hospital, going along to every single doctor's appointment. I'd cared for everything around the house—the laundry and the dishes and putting the boys to bed. And now she was saying it wasn't enough.

Why? What more could I give her?

Hearing her talk, seeing it in her eyes, I knew I had missed it. Somehow, I had done all that other stuff but still hadn't managed to love her as she needed to be loved. I took a deep breath. If we were going to rebuild our marriage, we had a long trek ahead of us.

"Is it possible?" I asked. "Can you love me again?"

"I don't know," she said. "But I'll try."

As I processed this conversation over the next few days and tried to wrap my mind around it all, I was smacked in the head with a dose of truth. Even though I loved her very much, part of why I had been working so hard to get her better was that I wanted to get on with my career. I didn't want to lose out on my own dreams because of her illness. I had been so selfish, and the truth of this reality hurt.

I realized that if this was where my drive for success had taken me, then I wanted no part of it. But I believed that experiencing both success and a healthy marriage were possible. So I began asking Angie for forgiveness and a second chance at a relationship with her. The key to moving forward was this: actions speak louder than words. I had to prove everything to her with what I did as well as what I said.

After that late-night conversation, the question, "Did I get to your heart?" became my checkpoint with Angie. Sometimes I asked it in fun or in jest, but most of the time I was serious. Getting to her heart became my new quest in life. And in the beginning, more often than not, she said something like, "You still don't get it, do you?"

For months, this was our barometer, our way of measuring progress. If we went out on a date or talked about her medical situation or if I gave her something special, I'd later ask, "Did I get to your heart?"

I slowly began learning her love language was quality time, not just asking her about her day but engaging with her in conversation about it.

We started being more intentional about spending time together, going on more fun dates and trying new things. One night we went to see a symphony, a first for both of us, and we enjoyed it so much that we stopped for dinner on the way home. We talked late into the night about the experience and what we learned.

As we sat there in the restaurant, snuggling on the same side of the booth like young love birds, we realized that we could still thrive off new, fun, spontaneous experiences. For us, that was one of the ways we could keep our love alive. This became one of the tools we used to rebuild our relationship.

It didn't happen overnight, but Angie started to appreciate the effort. And I started to understand her in ways I had never taken the time to figure out before. The things she appreciated the most weren't always things that came naturally to me. We quit making assumptions about the other person's motives and began rebuilding trust, reconstructing our relationship from the ground up, and even getting to the point where we could again make unified decisions.

As we did this, we started connecting on all levels.

We took a trip to Florida, just the two of us for eight days, and it was like our honeymoon on steroids. About four days in, we realized we were no longer talking about our boys and everyday life but engaging in meaningful conversations about each other. We were going deep. Intimacy came more naturally, connecting emotionally on a level we didn't know existed. We couldn't wait to touch and be around each other. Even sex was intimate and genuine, drawing us closer together as a couple.

We came home refreshed, glowing in love, and operating with renewed energy. The benefits for our marriage were so clear that we decided we would take a weeklong trip, just the two of us, every other year. We recently set up the details and dates for our next week-long getaway, and even though as I write this it's roughly 328 days away, we're already anticipating it like kids at Christmas.

One of the biggest areas for potential growth I confronted as I tried to win back my wife's heart involved my work/life balance.

Was it possible to leave work at work?

Could I come home to my family and my wife and be fully present with them?

Vacations were important, but we couldn't be on vacation all the time. Working some balance into normal life felt like the key to everything, and it became my central focus in restoring my relationship with Angie, becoming a better father, and putting myself on a path to sustainable success.

Finding this balance between work and family and maintaining it was the key to living the life I had always dreamed of. I went on a mission to figure out how to pull it off.

Chapter Six
Managing Work
Successfully

Before I embarked on this separation of work life and home life, I laid a strong foundation with my employer.

First of all, I worked hard. I pulled my weight. I didn't want my boss or my co-workers to have any doubts about my effort or commitment to the job.

I also increased the level of communication with my team. As I started making changes in how I worked, I kept my team aware of the situation so that they didn't feel ignored, left out, or surprised. Then, I followed through. I said what I did. I did what I said.

Finally, I focused on being detail-oriented. Doing my job right was key. If I sent people into the field and they thought they were fixing a toilet and it ended up being a faucet, I wasn't building respect and rapport. I was eroding their confidence in me. The details had to be right.

These things allowed me to begin to separate my work from the rest of my life. If I hadn't been a hard worker and gained the respect of my colleagues, if I hadn't communicated with them, if I hadn't followed through on issues that came up and made sure the details were right, this would not have worked.

With that foundation in place, I was ready to move forward in separating my work life from my home life.

This is what I committed to doing :

Turn off work emails outside of working hours.

In order to fully invest in your family and return to work refreshed, you need to mentally leave work. Emails and smart phones keep us engaged long after we have clocked out. Receiving or checking emails at home takes your attention away from your family relationships. It also gives us an excuse not to do our jobs well when we're at work because we always have a back-up plan: clean out the inbox at home.

This is a terrible idea for your family as well as your career.

This was not an easy transition for me. One Friday evening, I sat in my truck in the driveway outside our house, staring at the long weekend ahead. I grabbed my phone and, for the first time, I turned off my work emails. The first step in balancing my home and work life and moving towards the life I always wanted would be to leave work at work.

The reality was that I had to disconnect from work if I wanted to be present at home. Every time that little red number popped up on my cell phone telling me another work email waited in my inbox, it was a distraction. It was a distraction in the moment, and it remained a distraction, even if I didn't open it. When I did open it, my time and attention went into trouble-shooting and working out issues and not into the intense game of Chutes 'N Ladders or Candyland I was playing with my boys. If I checked my email and then had a conversation with Angie, I was still solving the work problem in my head. I simply couldn't be available for my family as they needed me to be if I was mentally still at work. The most logical thing to do was to cut work out of my mental space for the weekend.

Again, it wasn't easy. I'd come home Friday nights, and I'd sit in my truck for a couple minutes, wondering, "Am I really going to do this? Am I really going to turn off my work email? What if someone needs me? What if there's an emergency?"

Finally, I'd go to the settings and hit the button.

In the early days, I'd sometimes give in and check email on Saturday night. It probably took me five or six weeks to get to the point where I turned off my email on Friday afternoon at the office and then waited to turn it back on until I sat down at my desk on Monday morning.

Here's the thing: letting your work life invade your home life is not sustainable over the long-term. Your mind never gets a chance to shut down, to come back the next day refreshed and ready to tackle the big problems that need your attention. If you need extra motivation, my wife will tell you our relationship changed for the better when I quit checking emails 24/7. She saw I cared about her and our children, proving that work was not controlling my life.

I worked my tail off for my employer during the day then came home and chilled out with my family in my off hours. My wife and I could have more meaningful conversations because my mind wasn't cluttered with work problems, thanks to a continuous stream of email alerts. My employers won too because I showed up in the morning ready to take my game to a new level with a clear, refreshed mind.

It wasn't easy, but the battle was totally worth it. Try it. The benefits will blow your mind!

Complete your top three tasks at the beginning of each day.

We need to keep pushing ahead to complete the jobs we have in front of us. Dinner with our families and not checking email at home is important, but our jobs have to be done well. If we want our employers and co-workers to respect our boundaries, allowing us to take true time off, we need to impress with our production and work ethic.

By picking the top three things that need to be accomplished each day and completing them by noon, it gives me the flexibility I need to complete other goals as life happens around me. Plus, I get the satisfaction of a job well done, even if my afternoon gets out of control.

Without putting in a productive day's work, you'll find it's hard to disconnect at night because you still have work to do. Choose to finish the important things, and even if you have a to-do list waiting for you, you'll be amazed at how you can still relax at home in the midst of busy times. Learn to work hard during the day so you can relax guilt-free outside of work.

Eliminate personal distractions at work.

Think about all the time you waste at work doing 'your stuff' to kill time. No wonder we feel like working evenings and weekends is mandatory! Make it a point, starting today, to work when you're at work and to be at home when you're at home. In other words, be present. Things like personal emails, Facebook, or calling or texting friends are activities that keep you from being able to shut down when you leave work.

Find your distractions, and get an accountability partner to help you win at work. Your job and your family will thank you. And you'll thank yourself when quitting time rolls around and you're heading to the freedom of a 'no work zone.'

It's an amazing feeling; I have no idea how I survived in the past without it! Work becomes more fun and productive because you're now all in and killing it while you're there.

As incomprehensible as it might seem, when I stopped checking work emails at home, I became more productive at work. I took on more leadership roles and grew in the company. I never received any negative feedback about not checking email on the weekend. If there was a true emergency, people at work knew how to reach me. Our staff who worked on Saturday mornings knew that they could send me all the emails they needed and I'd get right to it on Monday morning.

The weekend thing worked. I was genuinely surprised I could have a life without working from Friday evening through Monday morning.

So I decided to try weekday evenings, too. This was an easier transition since it worked on the weekends without affecting my job and I saw how it benefited our family life. If I could pull it off, everything at home would go to another level. And it did. The mini-break each night gave me energy to go into the next day.

As a result of keeping work at work, Angie began to feel that I valued our family more than ever, that I was invested in our time together. She knew I had a lot going on at work every day, but she loved that I shut that off as soon as I got home. She felt more cared for, more important.

I was getting to her heart.

The next huge step was carrying this practice over into our vacations, and I decided no emails or cell phone during days off.

I grew up in an extremely hard-working community, one that sometimes places more value on hard work than on spending time with family. So how could this even be an option? The conventional wisdom often asks how crucial I actually am to the success of the company if I can go a week without someone at work needing me? If the business goes on when I'm not actively contributing, am I actually a valuable employee?

It was difficult to disconnect for an entire week during those first vacations, but I started enjoying it. Now, I can't imagine doing vacation any other way. The old way—spending six or seven hours on the beach but checking emails and voicemails on the phone every so often—doesn't even feel like a vacation anymore. That's not a sustainable way of getting a much-needed rest from work or taking a break.

That's not engaging in a vacation.

That's simply surviving it.

I know this is simple, but it's the core of what I used to get my life back.

Chapter Seven
Balancing It All

Life comes in seasons. There are seasons to your work/life balance. It's fluid, and that's precisely why it's so important to learn to balance these things.

The company I work for bought another company, and the whole transition happened while Angie and the kids were at the beach. It meant I was free to work evenings and put in some long days. Had my family been around, it would have meant a conversation about this temporary schedule. I might have picked up a couple nights a week or half days on Saturday just to get through this busy season.

Another time when things were crazy at work, I wrote up boundaries and emailed them to Angie and my boss. Among other things, I outlined the total hours I expected to work each week and if I worked past a certain time, I needed to buy supper on the way home. I also listed the benefits we could expect to get from my extra time and how long I anticipated this busy season to last. This brought clarity for everyone and gave us an opportunity to all be on the same page, maintaining realistic expectations both at work and at home. The project at work was a success, and I did not lose ground in my relationships at home.

This is all okay as long as it's a short-term thing. I don't want working evenings and weekends to become normal again, so we have to keep talking, and we have to push back when work threatens to take over the margins. It's a constant battle, a never-ending conversation. There's an ebb and flow—it's not one size fits all.

For the past three years, Angie and I have planned our year out in advance, and it's become a key to building the life we want. At first, it took some convincing before Angie was willing to try it. But she agreed, and we planned out the year together. After seeing it play out, she became a believer, and we have done it ever since.

We set aside time for us to review the upcoming year and lay out what is important to us, what family activities we want to do, and what work requirements we have. We ask if there is something we want to do individually. Once those questions are answered, we begin putting it on the calendar. When we're finished, we share it with anyone who might be involved.

This was our third year planning out the year, and organizing it ahead of time allowed us to spend seven weeks and five weekends at the beach. I took a four-day personal retreat; Angie went to a conference with her mom and sisters. The boys and I had our second annual dudes weekend. Angie and I spent two weekend-long dates with each other. She hosted a successful Christmas party for her home business, and I put in the work necessary to oversee the acquisition of a company while transitioning into a new role at work as general manager.

It was a good year.

Over a special dinner with Angie, watching the sun set over the water at the beach, she told me, "I'm now a true believer in planning out our year. We did all this in one year, and it wasn't even hard! It just happened! I never thought living such a fulfilled life could be so easy."

Daily journaling is another tool that's helped build this success. I use a template from Michael Hyatt to make it easy to capture things like how I'm feeling today, what I did yesterday, what I'm thankful for, and the one thing I need to do today. Journaling clears my mind, sets me up to make sure I'm getting my top three things done each day at work, and keeps me on track to hit my personal goals. It also helps me to recognize trends or patterns that could otherwise be written off as emotions, not facts.

Once, as I was writing down what I did the day before, it hit me that I had not recorded anything that moved the ball forward for a period of time. I was engulfed in the whirlwind and not fulfilling the needed tasks that would help me make progress. This gave me an opportunity to take inventory of my productivity and delegate a few tasks to others, and in a few days, I was back on track, moving in the right direction. Having the written record in front of me made it easier to spot the problem.

At this point, I only journal on workdays in the

morning. Find something that works for you. The simplicity of writing in a journal is huge, and if you can find the time of day and style that works best for you and stick with it, you'll be amazed at how your life will change for the better. For the first few months, I probably only journaled three to four times a week, and I changed a few things to personalize it. It took me three to six months to get this right and make it a habit. So don't give up on journaling, and keep fighting until you find your style.

Life Reimagined

Life Reimagined

Part Three
You Got This

Life Reimagined

Chapter Eight
The Benefits
Outweigh the Work

If you moved in with us now, you would see certain things happen on a daily basis because of these habits we have established, things we put in place and stuck with.

Have dinner together as a family.

Time together is precious and hard to come by for any family. We make it a point to have dinner together each night. It might only be 30-40 minutes, but it's valuable time spent interacting with our boys about school, their dreams, and what they're excited about.

It's a way we can teach them about growing up. Children grow so much through simple interactions, and it creates a time each day when we can regroup and enjoy each other's company, learning what's important to each person. This has given me an opportunity each day to connect with the important people in my life and to be reminded of what I love about them.

Make two-day, work-free weekends the norm.

We were not made to work seven days a week. This is your life and your family's life too, so find ways to enjoy it outside of the job. As a family, we look forward to weekends, but we look forward to Monday mornings too. We work hard during the week at school, at work, or at home, and then we can enjoy our weekend as a family.

I understand not everyone has weekends off, but the main key here is make sure you are truly taking off every week on the days you are not at work.

Weekends are so much fun at our house: lazy Saturday mornings, brunch as a family, an afternoon trip to do something fun together, church on Sunday, naps and games Sunday afternoon. This all fires us up to work hard during the week of work and school. It's a cycle we have embraced.

I discovered another revolutionary practice: sleeping in on Saturdays with my wife.

Of course, everyone has different opinions about sleeping in. "The early bird gets the worm" tends to be the prevailing attitude, especially in our culture and especially in the business world. But after trying this for a few weekends, I felt unexpectedly refreshed. I was sleeping in until 7 or 8 a.m., making breakfast, and simply spending time with my wife and sons. I didn't even think about work. Coming from my background, it almost felt morally wrong to have such downtime!

Work-free vacations.

Remember that week-long vacation Angie and I took to Florida? I did not take a single work-related phone call. I didn't know how many emails I was getting, and I didn't reply to any text messages; I even disconnected from social media. To ensure that Angie had my full attention, I guarded that week with my life.

It's not enough just to plan a trip and show up—you need to engage in it and set the proper boundaries to get the results you want. During the five weeks we spent at the beach this spring, I worked from the beach house each Friday while my family played in the sand. I knew what boundaries were in place, and I was dedicated to what we were trying to get out of that time away.

It's not a one-size-fits-all mentality—you don't have to do things the way I did. Be intentional about what you are doing on vacation, and at a minimum, completely shut down for at least one full week to recharge your batteries. You'll be blown away by the results when you do.

I recently listened to Cal Newport's book, *Deep Work*. He talks about the importance of boredom, white space, and how technology robs us of our future and our mental capacities. There is a problem when we are standing in line at the bank to deposit a check and we have to get our phone out! There's a problem when we can't stop at a red light without scanning our phone for any notifications. It's a problem when we get to the place where we need constant distraction; it takes away from time we might spend thinking up new ideas or considering new ways of living.

It takes work to break these habits in our lives, especially the ones that involve employment. Working is something our culture almost always respects, even if we do it when we should be doing something else. So at first you have to fill the time with other things—playing with your kids, exercising, picking up a hobby. I didn't just turn my emails off and become a different person. It was a two-year journey.

This is where I am: I've learned to turn off work, but I'm starting to rely on my phone for other ways to pass the time instead of playing hockey with the kids or going for a bike ride. It's a process; something that takes dedication, perseverance, and a willingness to constantly improve. I know I have to keep working at it.

Chapter Nine
Start Now

Start now.

Now is the time to start finding a work/life balance that works for you.

Now is the time to invest in those important relationships.

Don't put these things off for another day.

It's so important to understand your calling and utilize your gifts to the best of your ability. Even if your current job isn't your true calling, it can be an opportunity to excel in a way that will lead you to the next thing. Build knowledge where you are. Start working towards your true calling. Put some goals into place.

I built a life plan following the outline from *Living Forward* by Michael Hyatt and Daniel Harkavy. This plan has given me and my family so much clarity as well as the ability to move forward toward the end result we want, even if those around us don't always agree with our decisions.

Use whatever job you're currently in to create a new template for your life, one that will translate to the job of your dreams once you have it. I know many people who think, "Well, when I get the job of my dreams, I'm going to work evenings and weekends. I'm going to put everything into it."

Now is the time to start putting those parameters in place so that when you do get that "job of your dreams," you won't drown in it.

At this point in my life, I'm the general manager of the company where I work, a position that carries greater responsibility than I've ever had before. Plus, working on this book has taken a lot of effort, and I'm doing more with my family than I ever have before. My work hours have even expanded, within certain limits.

But I still have evenings at home.

I still have weekends at home with my family.

It's the only way I know how to do life now.

Creating a safe space where I could disconnect from work 100% was where the game changed for me. Not everyone has to do it exactly like this, but it's what worked for me, my job, my family, in my world.

You can do something.

In the middle of Angie's worst moments, when our marriage was nearly failing, when I didn't know how to move forward, Angie was praying. She told God, "I want my life to bring glory to you. This whole situation. And if this can bring glory to you, then I can endure it. Then, it would all be worth it."

In the same way, God is leading you through your unique life and experience for a reason. What has God given you a passion for? Because he's given you that intentionally. Don't be shy about who you are. Don't be ashamed of what you've been through. You have nothing to regret, nothing to hide. Share the victories. Share the struggles.

You owe it to the world.

You owe it to your family.

You owe it to yourself.

But you can never be your most effective when you're living in chaos.

You have to find balance in your life between

work, family, and other obligations.

You have to go deeper spiritually.

Now is the time to discover and live that other life, the one you've been longing for. You have what you need to build the foundations of a balanced, successful, faith-filled life.

Go and do it!

Leave chaos behind.

Find balance.

Thrive.

Acknowledgments

I'll never forget standing in the ER hallway beside Angie's bed, holding her hand, hoping for the best. I looked up and a familiar face walked around the corner: Matt, the CEO and owner of the company where I worked, had come to see how I was holding up and to let me know that he had canceled his plans to travel out of town on business, making it much easier for me to be in the hospital with my wife.

That's true leadership. That's building value in your team. That's helping a friend out. Some of the things I talk about in this book, I learned from Matt. We are both striving for the same quality of life while working hard to build a company without giving up on our dreams.

The team I have the privilege of working with every day is amazing. We watch out for each other. They stepped up while I helped my family heal and gave me grace as I learned how to live a balanced life. Hopefully, you work in a company that is as supportive of helping you work hard and play hard. If you do, congrats, that's a big first step, but you still need to work hard to build your own foundations and boundaries so you and your family can thrive.

If you do not work in a company that gives you this kind of flexibility, don't give up. Keep working hard and slowly implement things that help you live a well-rounded life. The things I share in this book will do wonders for your lifestyle. You have the opportunity to help create a new culture in your company, and once people see you working hard and playing hard, they will want to know your secret. It's only a matter of time.

Our families need a huge shout-out too. Angie's mom, sisters, and their families welcomed our two boys into their homes for a few months while Angie could not care for them. My family helped out with food that fit Angie's diet. Both of our extended families went out of their way to do what they could to help out around the house and encourage us. I'm forever thankful for everything they did during those tough, dark years. We were so blessed by family, friends, and our church family. There are too many stories to tell here—we'll save that for a future book. Thank you so much for caring for us. You all know who you are.

To the mentors and counselors who took time to walk with me: thanks so much. Your wisdom and encouragement made all the difference in helping me keep my chin up, battle through, and grow professionally and personally over the years. You helped me keep my sanity and clean up my personal life so I could grow in my professional life.

Angie, you're the best girl. I'm madly in love with you. You amaze me every day with how brave you were and still are. God brought us together to do great things and we are just starting on that journey. Your forgiveness, allowing me a second chance at gaining your trust, will never be forgotten. I'm sorry we never talked about my fear of losing out on my dreams due to your health so that we could grieve together—you were dealing with the same thing. I've learned so much, and at the top of the list is how blessed I am to have you as my wife. I'm looking forward to dating you for the rest of our lives and seeing where God takes us. I love you, Babes.

My prayer is that everyone who reads this book will take at least one action item, customize it to make it their own, and move one step closer to building the life of their dreams. It's possible and it's more amazing than you can imagine.

I was there in the chaos at one point. This was my story. I can't wait to hear your story someday soon.

Your friend on the journey,

Jason

READING LIST

These books have greatly influenced my journey and the writing of this book:

1. ***Essentialisim*** by Greg McKneown. Find out what is important, and do it well. Learn how to say no effectively.

2. ***How to Win Friends and Influence People*** by Dale Carnegie. People are important to success, and we need to treat them with respect in order to get the best results in relationships, both professionally and personally.

3. ***Rising Strong*** by Brene Brown. Rumble, reckon, learn to deal with the messy middle, and realize most people are not really attacking you but have fears in their own lives they need to protect. Life is messy but can also be fun and empowering when people are viewed properly and we keep ourselves in check, too.

4. ***Go Giver*** by John David Mann and Bob Burg. This is the story of how you can impact others by doing what you love and playing by a new set of rules that puts others first and makes you feel vulnerable at times but ultimately allows you to build the network needed to do great things.

5. ***Prayer*** by Tim Keller. How to build a real relationship with God, continue to press into Him, and search our hearts for what God is doing in our lives. I learned more about prayer journaling from this book than any other, and it changed the way I journal on a daily basis.

6. ***Deep Work*** by Cal Newport. The key to productivity is to remove distractions and embrace boredom so you can focus on the important work at hand and release the creativity in your mind. Being busy all the time limits our ability to focus on what is important. Do a few things well.

7. ***You and Me Forever*** by Francis and Lisa Chan. Details how marriage is designed to prepare us for the first time we meet God and our eternity with him. Through marriage, we get a view into eternity and why it is important to live every day that way and prepare our families to meet God.

8. ***Entreleadership*** by Dave Ramsey. This is the complete guide to how Dave runs his company. It's a comprehensive look at structure and leadership in a growing company.

9. ***The Secrets of Happy Families*** by Bruce Feiler. Thru interviewing people from all professions

of life, he is able to give good, useful advice on how to raise a family and make it fun for everyone while getting the results you are looking for.

10. ***The Compound Effect*** by Darren Hardy. How you can build a very successful life by doing the little things every day, compounding to huge results.

11. ***Living Forward*** by Daniel Harvakey and Michael Hyatt. How to build a plan so you can live the life of your dreams. This is a great book to refer to as you make decisions that will impact your life.

12. ***The Five Love Languages of Children*** by Gary Chapman. Children all need love in a different way.

Jason Ranck is married to Angie and they have two boys, Carter and Colton. He is the general manager at JM Lapp Plumbing and Heating. Continuing to learn from life, he has a strong passion to encourage leaders to live to their full potential, build flourishing families, and experience thriving careers. To learn more, visit www.jasonranck.com

Shawn Smucker is an author and co-writer passionate about creating and sharing good stories. He lives with his wife and six children in Lancaster, PA, where he helps people all around the world put their stories and passions into book form.